Summary Bundle: Ambition & Marriage | Readtrepreneur Publishing: Includes Summary of The Magic of Thinking Big & Summary of The Meaning of Marriage

By: David J. Schwartz

Proudly Brought to you by:

Legal & Disclaimer

Table of Contents

5

The Book at a Glance

The Magic of Thinking Big is designed for people who intensely desire success and are looking for ways to achieve it. First published in 1959, the principles and methods presented herein are still applicable and are guaranteed to get results.

Chapter 1 focuses on the power of belief and how to develop it. There are real-life stories of people who succeeded in their endeavors by simply believing that they could. After reading this chapter, you will be convinced that you, too, you can achieve great things if you believe.

"Excusitis" is a disease which drags many people into failure. Find out if you have it and learn how to immunize yourself against it by following the tips presented in Chapter 2.

In Chapter 3, you will learn how to destroy the number one enemy of success through action and confidence.

By adhering to the five simple steps presented in this chapter, you will be able to develop confidence.

The aim of this book is to show you that thinking big is the secret to success; the size of your thinking determines how big your achievements can be. Chapter 4 shows you how to measure your thinking size. It also teaches you how to develop the big thinker's vocabulary and vision.

Chapter 5 deals with creative thinking. Here, you will learn how to fight the worst enemy of creativity, enhance your creative strength, and harness the potential of your ideas.

Many people do not realize that what they are outside is a reflection of their thoughts. In Chapter 6, you will find the techniques that will make other people see what you want them to see in you. You will learn how to be important and gain the respect that you deserve.

Your environment largely influences the size of your achievement. Chapter 7 presents key points that will help you create an environment that works for your benefit.

Your attitude is another determinant of the size of your success. Learn the attitudes that will make you win people and develop a habit that is guaranteed to bring success in Chapter 8.

In order to achieve success, you need the support of other people. To gain this, you must have the right thinking toward others. The principles presented in Chapter 9 will show you how.

Chapter 10 shows the importance of the action habit. It demonstrates why waiting for the perfect moment and taking time to get ready keep you from achieving success. Learn how to develop the action habit in this chapter.

Everyone will experience setbacks at some point. Chapter 11 teaches you what to do with defeat when you encounter it and why it should not keep you from thinking big.

In Chapter 12, you will learn why it is important to have a clear vision of your goal. You will also discover how your desires can give you the energy and enthusiasm to work on your goal.

Finally, because success goes hand in hand with leadership, you will learn the four rules that will make you an effective leader in Chapter 13.

FREE BONUSES

P.S. Is it okay if we overdeliver?

Here at Readtrepreneur Publishing, we believe in overdelivering way beyond our reader's expectations. Is it okay if we overdeliver?

Here's the deal, we're going to give you an extremely condensed PDF summary of the book which you've just read and much more...

What's the catch? We need to trust you... You see, we want to overdeliver and in order for us to do that, we've to trust our reader to keep this bonus a secret to themselves? Why? Because we don't want people to be getting our exclusive PDF summaries even without buying our books itself. Unethical, right?

Ok. Are you ready?

Firstly, remember that your book is code: **"READ105"**.

Next, visit this link: **http://bit.ly/exclusivepdfs**

Everything else will be self explanatory after you've visited: **http://bit.ly/exclusivepdfs.**

We hope you'll enjoy our free bonuses as much as we enjoyed preparing it for you!

Preface

Several years ago, the author witnessed a sales meeting of a company's marketing representatives. The vice president, wanting to drive a point, presented the organization's top representative who earned five times more than the average earnings of the others despite being just about average in many aspects. Harry, the leading representative, was not smarter, nor did he work harder. He wasn't more educated and his health condition was the same as the others. According to the executive, the difference was that Harry thought five times bigger. And the size of his thinking, not his brain, was what brought him success.

The author was intrigued by this idea and dug deeper into what was behind the success of many people. He was able to prove that there is magic in thinking big.

However, most people do not seem to think that way. And with this kind of environment, you are influenced to limit your thinking. The idea that there are no more opportunities to lead or that there is too much competition for the top spots are forced into your mind, even though leaders themselves would contradict this. You are pushed to believe that you can't control your future and that you should let go of your dreams of a better life. People with petty minds convince you that success isn't worth the price.

The basic principles and concepts of this book are supported by the finest and biggest thinkers who lived throughout Earth's history. Intellectual minds like the prophet David, Ralph Waldo Emerson, John Milton, and William Shakespeare believed in the power and might of thinking. Their ideas, which are the basis of the steps laid down in this book, have been proven by several people who achieved successful and happy lives by thinking big.

The fact that you're reading this book reflects two admirable qualities: you are interested in success and you have the desire to look for the tools you need to achieve your goals. These qualities are necessary to reap real profits from this book.

Think big for a bigger life. Start right now and see how this will bring magic for you.

What This Book Will Do for You

Every chapter of this book contains practical concepts, methods, and ideologies that will help you utilize the power of thinking big. This book will explain you how you can...

Cultivate the power of belief, get big results, and succeed

Defeat the negative power created by disbelief

Learn how to heal from health, intelligence, age, and luck 'excusitis,' the failure disease

Learn how to build your confidence and conquer your fear of others

Develop and strengthen your creative power to do more and better

Know what you want in life to construct your ten-year goal

Train your mind to think, and discover why thinking is more important than knowledge

Measure your thinking size and find out how it relates to your success

Learn how to think big and utilize your ideas

Discover how to think, feel, and be important

Create a work and life environment that operates to your advantage

Develop the attitudes that will help you achieve what you want

Earn more money by having a service-first attitude

Become more likeable and build friendships

Know why you should only think well of others and use this to win their support

Learn how to manage and learn from every setback and remember that this should not keep you from thinking big

Decide to work on your ideas NOW and not later when circumstances are perfect

Build yourself by getting into the habit of speaking up

Set defined goals that will help you accomplish things

Understand the four rules of leadership

Think towards, believe in, and push for progress

Tap the power of thinking big in life's most critical situations

Chapter 1: Believe You Can Succeed and You Will

People define success in different ways. Success could be measured by wealth, admiration and respect one's social and business life, lack of failure, or happiness and contentment. Success can also mean achieving your goals in life. And who wouldn't want success?

Our beliefs teach us that faith can move mountains. And if you really believe, you can do so. Most people doubt that they could do such a thing; these are the people who mistake belief with wishful thinking. But you can never wish a mountain away. Only by believing that you could do it will you gain success.

Belief develops a positive attitude towards your goals. If you believe you can do something, you will put time and effort to do it.

Every young person who enters the workforce wishes that someday he or she would be successful. But many young adults think that climbing the ladder of success is impossible, and so they do not try, instead settling for being average.

However, a few people do not just wish, but believe that they can achieve success. By studying and understanding the attitudes and behaviors of their superiors, they learn how successful people handle their problems and make decisions.

If you believe you can, you will know how.

A few years ago, a young woman decided to start a business selling mobile homes. She didn't have any experience in managing a business. Her savings were way below the required capital. Many people advised her that she couldn't and shouldn't do it.

In spite of these naysayers, she believed in herself. She admitted her lack of money and experience, but did her research. The mobile home industry was going to expand. She knew that she would do better in marketing trailers than any of her competitors.

She was able to raise the capital she needed. She gained the confidence of two investors with her unfailing belief that she could succeed. And finally, she got a manufacturer to supply her with a limited stock of trailers without paying any money.

She sold millions of dollars' worth of trailers in her first year, and expects to double that amount the following year.

Your belief will not only lead your mind to figure out how to accomplish things; a strong belief in yourself will also make people trust you.

*

Twenty-one engineering firms were asked to submit a proposal to design bridges that would cost five million dollars. Whichever company was chosen would earn a 4% commission. The four largest firms immediately accepted it. Of the 17 small companies, only one was not discouraged by the size of the project. And guess what, they won despite having only three engineers.

Great results and the achievement of things once thought impossible are the products of belief.

People who failed in their businesses or careers had one thing in common: they didn't think their venture would work out. And this attitude led to their failure.

Disbelief in one's mind draws reasons to support this negative power.

An ambitious young writer compared herself to another writer and believed that she would never be nearly as successful as him. She was not aware that this author didn't have exceptional talent — he only writes well because he believes that he is one of the best writers.

Believe that you have the capacity to surpass your idols. Observe and learn from the people you admire and you will be able to do better. Your thoughts shape you — how you see yourself influences how other people regard you. Believe that you can do big things, that you are worth a lot, and that you are important.

*

A good example of making your mind work for you can be seen in this example of a Detroit businessman. This man used to make a decent living working in the tool-

and-die trade, but he knew that him and his family deserved better.

The night before a job interview, he pondered his failure. He listed the names of five people he knew who were doing better than him in terms of money and job responsibility. He realized that none of them had a superior intellect or integrity, nor did they possess better education or personal habits. But he lacked one quality of success — initiative. He believed that he wasn't worth much. And that's why he had been selling himself short.

Realizing his weakness and how his mind had worked against him, he decided that he had had enough of feeling second-class. With renewed confidence in himself, he summoned the courage to ask $3,500 more than what he was previously earning. He got the job and later on established a positive reputation in the industry.

Good things happen to those who believe in themselves.

*

Imagine your mind as a thought factory, continuously producing countless thoughts each day, and responsible for the operations of the factory are two people — Mr. Triumph and Mr. Defeat. As the name implies, Mr. Triumph is in charge of producing positive thoughts, while Mr. Defeat oversees the generation of negative thoughts. Both men work really hard.

Your mind is a thought factory, producing countless thoughts each day powered by you. If you feed your mind with a negative thought, it will work on producing reasons to prove that you are right. Similarly, telling yourself positive things leads to a mind that produces pleasant thoughts.

Keep feeding your mind positive things and it will work to produce ideas on how you can succeed.

The US population is growing at a record rate. New consumers mean new industries, scientific breakthroughs, and expanding markets. This spells more opportunities for top-level positions in every field. You can be one of these leaders.

Think of all these opportunities as rewards. With your mind believing that you can succeed, you will learn ways to get whatever you want.

How to Develop the Power of Belief

1. Always think of success. Do not allow thoughts of failure to conquer your mind.

2. Believe in yourself and what you do. You are better than what your mind tells you.

3. Have the courage to believe big. That is the only way to achieve big success.

Successful people religiously follow a plan for self-development and growth. This book should be a part of your plan. It will provide you with ideas of what-to-do and how-to-do-it. And most importantly, it works.

Chapter 2: Cure Yourself of Excusitis, the Failure Disease

"Excusitis" is the mind-killing disease that plagues unsuccessful people. Those who live mediocre lives will never run out of excuses. Successful people, on the other hand, could have used the same excuses made by second-rate men, but chose not to.

Constant repetition of either positive or negative thoughts will cause them to grow. Because of this, excusitis will only get worse. At first, excuses are just lies, but once people become accustomed to using excuses to explain their predicaments, they start to believe that these excuses are the real reasons why they are not advancing in their lives.

Hence, the first step to make your thinking work for your success is to immunize yourself against excusitis.

The Four Most Common Forms of Excusitis

1. Health Excusitis

Many people use health issues as an excuse for why they fail at making more money, performing great responsibilities, or achieving success.

No one on earth is perfectly healthy. While many will succumb to this defense, people who are inclined to thoughts of success will not. Success-thinking individuals will always be optimistic and see health issues as obstacles that have to be conquered.

Four Things You Can Do to Kick Health Excusitis

1. Avoid discussing your health problems. Talking about it can actually make you feel worse.

2. Keep yourself from worrying about health.

3. Appreciate your health condition. It could be a lot worse, but it isn't. Being thankful can protect you from acquiring more troubles.

4. Enjoy your life. Don't make your health an excuse for not making something out of your life.

2. Intelligence Excusitis

Most people think that they need to have powerful brains in order to succeed. And many tend to misjudge their intelligence.

When it comes to success, your level of intelligence shouldn't be considered such an important factor. What's more important is how you use what you have. Make your thinking guide your intelligence. A person with an average IQ that possesses the right attitude can become a better leader and make more money than a genius who uses his brain to make up reasons that prove that his ideas won't work.

Three Ways to Cure Intelligence Excusitis

1. Remember that your brain is more powerful than what you think. Focus on what you have and use it.

2. Cultivate a positive and winning attitude. It is more important than intelligence.

3. Be creative. Your mind should think of new ideas and techniques rather than store unimportant facts.

3. Age Excusitis

Your age should not be a hindrance to achieve your goals. You are never too young or too old to do what you want to do. You are always at the right age to pursue opportunities.

How to Handle Age Excusitis

1. View your current age positively. Don't think that you are too old to be productive or too young for great responsibilities.

2. A person's productive life starts in the early 20s and could last beyond his or her 70s. If you are suffering from age excusitis, consider how old you are. Think of how many years of productivity you have spent. You will be surprised at how much time you actually have left.

3. Adopt the mindset of successful people. It is not too late for you to start doing things that interest you. Start now and your best years will be ahead of you.

4. Luck Excusitis

A lot of people believe their problems are caused by bad luck. These are the same people who see success as a case of good luck. People who succumb to this disease fail to recognize that in order to achieve success, they have to persevere with the right approach.

Conquer Luck Excusitis in Two Ways

1. Remember that there is no such thing as luck — everything happens for a reason. Don't blame luck if someone is doing better than you. A coworker who got promoted or closed a massive deal didn't achieve that feat because of luck; it involved hard work, careful planning, effective execution and the correct attitude.

2. Nurture winning qualities. Success is won, not handed down. You can't simply wish for luck to be on your side. You have to make an effort and master the values needed to become successful.

Chapter 3: Build Confidence and Destroy Fear

Fear is real, and in order to defeat it, you must first recognize its existence.

Fear is the number one enemy of success. Fear of failure prevents a person from taking advantage of opportunities. Fear of embarrassment prevents someone from opening his mouth. Uncertainty and lack of confidence keep many people away from achieving great things.

To treat your fear, remember that no one is born confident. Every single bit of a person's confidence is acquired.

This chapter will show you how to build confidence.

*

The cure for fear is action. You will not learn how to swim if you don't jump into the water. Failure to act feeds fear.

There was once a sales executive who feared losing his job due to poor performance. Believing that there's nothing he could do, he merely hoped for the best. It didn't keep him from worrying though. Hope is good, but it is nothing without action.

The executive followed the advice he was given. He talked with his managers to give him time to find and execute solutions. He made a special sale to clear slow-moving products. He started meeting his staff daily instead of weekly to boost their enthusiasm. It took months of hard work but he was able to improve his performance and secure his job.

Improve your appearance if it embarrasses you. Make service better to keep an important customer who is losing confidence in you. If you are dreading an examination, study harder. Don't spend all your time worrying about things that are out of control. Divert your thoughts and concentrate on matters you could work on. Take actions to conquer your fear.

*

Self-confidence, or the lack of it, can be a result of how memories are handled. For effective management, you should only hold on to positive memories. Unsuccessful people dwell on their unpleasant thoughts; successful people don't. Furthermore, only by utilizing encouraging thoughts will you gain confidence. Approaching a situation with negative thoughts, like memories of failure or inferiority, will make you feel incapable.

One of the biggest fears of many people is other people. To put other people in a proper perspective, remember these two things: 1) view others as your equal and be understanding of them — if you are in a meeting with someone you consider important, keep in mind that you are important as well, and 2) when someone declares war on you, let him fire first and forget about it.

*

Guilt is a confidence-killer. You feel guilt when you commit actions which go against your conscience. This

33

feeling disrupts your thought process. You keep worrying that people would eventually find out about your weakness, and if they do, they'd lose their confidence in you.

Thinking yourself to success means doing what's right to preserve your confidence. Your actions directly affect your emotions. If you act confidently, you will also think confidently. But how do you build confidence? Below are five exercises that will help you:

1. Always sit at the front. People who sit at the back of the room lack confidence because they are afraid of being seen.

2. Make eye contact. If you avoid meeting other people's eyes, they will think that you're hiding something or that you're feeling inferior.

3. Walk faster. Increasing your pace by 25% is ideal. Improve your posture as well.

4. Speak up. The more you keep your mouth shut, the more inadequate you will feel. Speaking up will make it easier to speak up the next time.

5. Smile, even when you're feeling low. Smiling widely and sincerely will not only ease your negative emotions, it can cheer others up as well.

Chapter 4: How to Think Big

It is surprising that there are many people who think small. Success is measured by the size of one's thinking. And only those who think big attain great achievements.

Measuring your thinking size involves two steps. First, identify your five main strengths. You could do this yourself or with the help of objective people. Second, under each of your strengths, write the names of successful people who aren't as proficient in this strength are yourself.

After this exercise, you will realize that you have better qualities than other successful people. Now that you know that you're bigger than you thought you were, you should start thinking as big as you really are.

Four Ways to Develop the Big Thinker's Vocabulary

Big thinkers use optimistic words to produce positive images not only in their minds but in the minds of others. Below are ways to develop this quality:

1. When asked about how you feel, reply with positive and cheerful words. A person who is known for always feeling great can easily win friends.

2. Use these same words to describe other people, especially with absent third parties. People will eventually find out if you talk ill of them, and that will only hurt you.

3. Encourage others using positive speech. Sincerely compliment a person who deserves it at every opportunity.

4. State your plans using positive words. When faced with a difficult task, tell people that this is a great opportunity for them to prove themselves instead of compelling them to work because they have no other choice.

See What Can Be, Not Just What Is

Big thinkers focus more on what is possible. They look beyond the present situation. The examples below demonstrate how you can develop this view.

1. Make things worth more. Think of value-adding ideas. A run-down house in a barren field is a tough sell. But one realtor specializing in rural properties can make a lot of money from it by selling not the farm itself but the idea of what it can be.

For example, he may propose to convert a farm near a growing city into a riding stable. People's love for the outdoors means that more money allotted for recreation. With a clear and convincing plan, he can easily sell the property at a higher price than previously quoted.

2. Value people. Many salespersons tend to measure a customer's worth based on a single sale. A first-time spender who pays little is usually valued little and not given a top-notch service. What salespeople fail to realize is a customer's potential expenditure, from which

they can benefit only if they make him or her a regular customer. Valuing a customer through excellent service will keep him or her coming back.

3. Make yourself worth more. Even if you're content where you are, ask yourself regularly how you can make yourself better. Visualize how much more valuable you can be, and you will come up with ways to realize your potential.

*

Thinking big is a proven way to achieve great heights. Take the story of 30-year old Harry, for example. After working at a medium-sized company as an accountant for about four years, he succeeded the owner-manager. His secret? He is a big thinker.

Not only did Harry focus on his tasks, he was also genuinely interested in the company. He came up with ideas that improved the company's operations. He helped new employees get used to their positions. He did all this even when there was no direct benefit.

Merely doing your job is not enough. Treat yourself as part of the team, of the company, and you will start thinking that your company's achievement or loss is yours as well. You will see yourself sincerely invested, which is the attitude that makes a great leader.

But many potential leaders and achievers let petty things obstruct their road to success. Petty thoughts turn a simple misunderstanding to a full-blown quarrel. Minding even the smallest things such as the size of one's office or cubicle, can lead to poor performance at work.

Don't let the little things hold you back. Apply these steps to help you manage your thoughts about trivialities.

1. Stay focused on the big objective. You can win a battle, but still lose the war. Always aim for the big things.

2. Before acting negatively at something, ask yourself if it really matters. Don't waste your time and energy over

petty things. Trivialities shouldn't be a source of frustration.

3. Don't let trivialities entrap you. In whatever you do, think of the aspects that are more important and concentrate on them.

Chapter 5: How to Think and Dream Creatively

A creative thinker discovers new ideas and approaches in doing things. Being able to do things better will lead you to success. So how do you boost your ability to think creatively?

Go back to the idea of belief. If you believe that you can move a mountain, you will. Your mind will be conditioned to look for ways that will help you achieve your goals. But if you think that something is not attainable, your mind will find reasons that will prove you are right. Really believing that something can be done is fundamental to creative thinking.

If you want to cultivate your creative strength through belief, do these two things:

1. Erase the word "impossible" from your vocabulary.

2. Think of one thing you want to achieve but deem impossible. List down reasons why you can make it

possible and focus only on them, not why you considered it impossible in the first place.

The worst enemy of creative thinking is traditional thinking. Those who abide with this are bound to get stuck in a rut. They employ old ways that they believe work for them. These people are afraid of change and the risks related to it. They may get things done but they don't improve.

The only constant thing is change. Techniques that work today may not be applicable anymore tomorrow. You need to invent and re-invent. You need to have a creative mind in order to keep up with this fast-changing world.

Here are some ways to fight traditional thinking which hinders you from harnessing creativity:

1. Be like a sponge. Absorb and welcome new ideas. Don't assume that it won't work unless you've tried it.

2. Try something new each day. Don't let yourself be trapped in a routine, be it at work, home, or life in

general. Foster an interest in other aspects related to your job to prepare you for more responsibilities.

3. Be a forward-thinker. Always think of how to be better, not how to maintain the status quo. Accept change and strive for progress.

We all know that perfection is unattainable. Hence, there will always be a room for improvement. Each day, ask yourself how you can do better and how you can be better; eventually, you will find ways that will lead to your success.

*

Now that you know you can do better, ask yourself, "Can I do more?"

Your ability to do more depends on how much you think you could do. When you believe that you can accomplish more than the tasks you have at hand, your mind will work on finding the way for you.

In whatever you do, the formula for success is doing better and doing more. If you are given the chance to do more at work, take it as a compliment. With bigger responsibility, your value increases.

*

Your creativity can be enhanced through asking and listening to what others have to say. Top leaders spend more time seeking advice rather than offering it. Below are three steps to nurture your creative mind through asking and listening.

1. Persuade other people to talk. Listen to what they have to say. By doing so, you can have more inputs that can assist your creativity. The more you give other people the chance to speak up, the more they will like you and you can make more friends.

2. Ask for suggestions. Your idea may be good but it won't hurt to let other people refine it. You can end up with something much better.

3. Don't just listen. Concentrate and understand what the other person is saying. Let his idea seep into your mind.

Ideas are nothing if they are not put into action. You can have great ideas but you can only use them for your advantage if you know how to harness their potential. To develop your idea, follow these steps:

1. Whenever an idea comes up, make sure you write it down. Don't trust your memory to keep it for you.

2. Store your ideas and regularly evaluate them. Eliminate those that have no use anymore.

3. Make your idea grow by relating it with other ideas. Learn more about it. And when it's ready, you can make it work for yourself.

Chapter 6: You Are What You Think You Are

Have you ever wondered why one person treats someone differently from another? Like when a man will open a door for certain women and not others? The answer is thinking. Other people see you the way you see yourself. What you think you deserve, other people will give you.

Your actions reflect your thoughts. If you think you are average, you will act average. On the other hand, if you think you are important then you will act important.

Remember that how you think controls how you act, and how you act influences how others treat you. In order to gain respect, you have to believe that you deserve it. Respect yourself first and other people will do the same.

Read on to know how you can increase self-respect.

Look Important – It Helps You Think Important

Your appearance says a lot of things about you. Being well-dressed tells others that you are an important person, reliable, smart, and that you have great things going on. These attributes command respect from other people. A person who dresses shabbily suggests negative things such as laziness, incompetence, and sloppiness. This is the kind of person who is ignored and belittled.

Appearance affects thinking. A soldier will only feel he is a true soldier when he is in uniform. If you look important, you will be able to think important. If you want to be successful, you have to look successful.

Think Your Work Is Important

Your attitude towards your work determines how you do your job. If you consider it important, you will always do your best. And when you give your best, you will achieve great results which equates to more money, promotion, and respect from your employers.

To be successful in any endeavor, you must work enthusiastically. You can only develop enthusiasm if you think that what you are doing is important. Being passionate produces excellent work. Your disposition will also influence other people around you, leading to outstanding performance in the workplace.

Give Yourself a Peptalk Several Times Daily

If you are faced with problems, tell yourself that you can surpass them. Many people choose to beat themselves with negativity. They think of failures instead of finding solutions. Instead of finding courage, they dwell on fear. Don't be one of them.

Before you can sell yourself to others, you first have to sell yourself to yourself. Identify your best qualities and assets, and write them down. At least once a day, stand in front of a mirror and read them out loud. Say it with a lot of willpower. Read them before you tackle challenging situations. Read them when you're feeling low. Read them whenever you need courage.

Upgrade Your Thinking. Think Like Important People Think

Your thoughts become your actions. And when you upgrade your thinking, your actions improve, leading to success.

When something bothers you, ask yourself if successful people will worry about that thing. Read books, articles, or journals which successful people read. Are you using the vocabulary of important people? Is your appearance comparable to theirs? What would they do with the ideas that you have?

In every situation, think and act like important people do.

Chapter 7: Manage Your Environment: Go First Class

Imagine growing up in another country. Do you think your dress style, occupation, hobbies, and behavior would be the same as they are now? Of course not. Different environments exert different influences which shape you in a totally different person.

Your habits and your preference in food, music, and entertainment are all affected by the environment in which you grew up. The size of your thinking, goals and ambitions are also largely guided largely by the environment.

Your environment perpetually affects you. What you will be in the years to come depends on what you surround yourself with. You are constantly changing so you should make your environment work for your fulfilment and success.

Recondition Yourself for Success

As children, we dreamt big. Our goals were set high. We planned to become leaders, innovators, rich and famous, and the best in whatever field we chose. But even before we reached the age when we could start working on our goals, we were brainwashed. Negative things were thrown at us. We were made to believe that we would fail, so we shouldn't bother trying.

This brainwashing made many people totally give up. These are the ones who completely believed that they couldn't achieve greatness. They settled into mediocre jobs, trying to convince people that they are happy even though deep inside they are longing for something better.

There are people who started adulthood thinking that they had a chance at success. But after some time, they developed fears of defeat, uncertainty, and competition, which convinced them that success wasn't worth the effort.

Finally, there is a small group who didn't surrender. And they are the ones who are the happiest because they have achieved the most.

Everyone wants to be part of the third group. But in order to do so, you have to fight all the negativity cast at you. You can't allow other people's pessimistic opinion poison your mind.

Make It a Rule to Seek Advice from People Who Know

Successful people are willing to give help, so approach them. Go first class whenever you search for answers. Follow these simple steps to make your environment first class.

1. Expand your network. Make new friends. Become a member of an organization. Go to places where you can meet a variety of people. Socializing in new groups prevents boredom and dullness and gives you a broader understanding of people while nourishing your mind.

2. Make friends with people who are different from you. Get to know people whose opinions are different from

53

yours, and interact with people with different faiths and political views. However, make sure that these people have the same outlook as yours in terms of success.

3. Select friends who rise above trivialities and are interested in positivity. Find and keep those who genuinely want to see you succeed. Associating yourself with petty thinkers would only gradually turn you into one.

*

A lot of people take part in gossip. While many think that it is harmless, negative talk about other people can do a lot of damage. Gossip is a thought poison. It makes you focus on petty things. There is nothing right about gossip.

Conversations are natural functions of your environment and they take a huge chunk of it. Talking about your plans and aspirations make you feel alive. Conversations build relationships. Talking about others is not unhealthy if it is kept positive.

*

In everything you do, always go first class. Pay for quality goods and services. Keep in mind that you get what you pay for. And if the thought of not being able to afford firstclass discourages you, remember that first class is the only way. Choose quality over quantity. People evaluate you for quality, deliberately or not. First class may cost a lot upfront, but in the long run, it can cost no more than second class.

Chapter 8: Make Your Attitudes Your Allies

Our thoughts are expressed through our actions. Our attitudes reflect our thinking. You can read someone's mind by studying his behavior and appearance. You can also tell a lot about a person's attitude by the way he talks and what he says.

Your attitude determines what and how big you can accomplish. With the right attitude, you can win people, make a good leader and have a happy life. You can succeed in everything.

Grow the I'm-Activated Attitude

You reap what you sow; results are relative to the amount of work you devoted. You can't motivate others to do their best if you're not enthusiastic. In order to develop your enthusiasm, follow these three steps:

1. Make an effort to know more. Your disinterest towards something is due to your lack of knowledge about it. Enthusiasm grows when you dig deeper.

2. Do everything with life. Show your teeth when you smile. Always give firm handshakes. Be sincere and positive in whatever you say. Be bold when you tell yourself you can do it and you will.

3. Disseminate good news. Remember that how you feel is a reflection of how you think you feel. Sharing good things, like feeling great, will actually make you feel a lot better. Good news also excites and encourages people. Therefore, broadcasting good news isn't only good for you, it makes other people feel better as well.

Grow the You-Are-Important Attitude

It is a fact that every single person wants to feel valued. The need to feel important is natural for a human being.

Your success depends on how important you feel and how you make others feel the same way. When you show someone that he is important to you, he will be willing to do more for you. And someone you help to feel that he is valuable will do the same thing for you. Here's what you should do to develop the you-are-important attitude:

1. Be grateful. Make it a point to let people know that you appreciate what they do for you. Tell them how they are important to you. Practice gratitude with sincerity and personalized praises. Compliment people not only for big accomplishments but also for the little things. Treat every person with importance, no matter where they are in life.

2. Call people by their names. Pronounce them properly and spell them correctly. Making a mistake on someone's name will make him or her feel that he or she is not important to you. Add the appropriate title to address every person you are not familiar with. Titles may mean nothing to you but others consider it a boost.

3. Give credit where credit is due. Recognize the efforts of others. Personally complimenting people will encourage them to accomplish more.

Want to Make Money? Then Get the Put-Service-First Attitude

The desire to make money is completely normal and does not reflect greed. Having money means being able to give your family and yourself a good life. Money is essential if you want to help the needy. You need money to live a full life.

The amount of money you make depends on how much you value service. Customers will value you and keep coming back if you offer quality service. Your company will not pay you more if you simply promise better performance. You will only get a raise by demonstrating that you are worth more, which is seen in great work.

To cultivate this attitude, go beyond others' expectations of you. Put service first and money will come to you.

Chapter 9: Think Right Toward People

Success is brought about by collaborative effort. An executive, a college dean, or a politician, you rely on the support of other people. In order to achieve success, you can't avoid depending on others. But how do you win people's support?

The simple answer is to think right toward other people. This chapter demonstrates how it is done.

1. Make an effort to be liked by other people. Many times, amicability can determine whether you get the job or promotion. You may think this is unfair. But ask yourself, would people will be encouraged to work hard for someone they don't like?

Remember this — to rise to the top, you need to be lifted up by people who like you. The more likeable you are, the easier it is for other people to endorse you.

2. Build friendships and take the initiative to do so. Waiting for others to make the first move is like ignoring them, which isn't the right mentality. In addition, it is not a leader's approach in establishing relations.

To win friends, grab every opportunity you get to introduce yourself. Make sure you get people's names, and that they do the same for you. Find out their details. E-mail or call them. Follow through if you really want to know people.

However, do not try to buy friendship. If you do, you only lose money and gain hatred.

3. Realize that each person is unique in his or her own way. Accept this fact and the right to be different. You may even find one person who virtually doesn't share any similarities with you. A person's different preference, lifestyle, and religious or political views should never be a reason for you to dislike him or her. Furthermore, don't impose your beliefs and principles on others and don't try to change them.

Don't expect perfection from other people and accept that everyone has limitations. Do not cast out someone because of a single mistake. You may be a lot better than others but this does not make you perfect.

4. Always find the good in people. Thinking right towards others is finding a quality to like even in a person who is detested by everyone. Do not let other people's judgment influence how you see a person.

Imagine a situation when a higher-up praises your work but also points out that you can still improve. The wrong mindset will focus on him being a critic trying to find faults in everything you do. But a properly managed mindset will remember that higher-up as someone who is interested in seeing you grow and improve.

5. Do not monopolize a conversation. Successful people love to listen to others as much as they love to talk. Encourage others to talk about themselves and share their views and ideas.

Being generous during conversations will not only win you friends, it also helps you know more about others.

And by learning more about others, you will have the opportunity to influence them.

6. Always be courteous. Good manners keep you from frustrations and stress.

You will know if you have really mastered the right way of thinking toward people when you maintain a positive mindset even when things don't go your way. If you focus on how to do things better and improve yourself rather than on blaming and resenting the people who impeded your victory, you have passed the test.

Chapter 10: Get The Action Habit

Most people don't know that all leaders agree on one thing — there is a big need for competent people to hold key positions in all fields. However, most candidates are only almost qualified; they lack one essential quality — the ability to produce results.

A creative mind is important. But great ideas will have no value unless you act upon them. Take action. Make something out of your great idea in order to achieve success.

*

Just like people, conditions will never be perfect. One of the biggest mistakes people make when they want to start something is waiting for the perfect moment. If you wait for something that will never come, you will find yourself waiting forever.

Fear of problems and difficulties keeps a person from springing into action. But remember that in every endeavor you take, there will always be risks. Imagine yourself planning on driving to another city on the condition that everything should be perfect and that you would face no risk. You could never have the assurance that you wouldn't have to take any detours, or that there wouldn't be any reckless drivers on the road. If you wait for these risks to disappear, you will not be going anywhere, literally.

What you can do as a success-oriented person is to face these difficulties. You will never be able to totally eliminate risks but you can reduce them, prepare for them, and think of solutions to resolve all possible obstacles.

*

Postponement is the cousin of waiting-for-the-perfect-moment. Many people commit the mistake of choosing to work on their dreams in the near future. Later becomes tomorrow. Tomorrow becomes next week, next month or never. If you want to get things accomplished, take action now.

Taking time to get ready is one of the reasons why people prefer to act later. You may be able to relate to this scenario. Joe, a typical college student is trying to write a paper. He decides to have dinner first while watching videos so he won't be hungry when he starts writing. By the time he finishes eating, he is so invested in the video series that he watches some more videos. A few hours later, he realizes he really needs to start working on his paper but now cannot focus because he's stressed by the time constraint. He is able to finish his paper but it is of poor quality.

Joe's mistake was spending too much time in preparation, which is something too many people do. To free yourself from this trap, remind yourself that you will not achieve anything by postponing. Instead of getting ready, get going.

*

Leaders want people who not only have the ability to come up with new and ambitious ideas but the initiative to make them happen as well. Initiative is doing the right thing without being told. Having initiative will place you high above others.

To foster a habit of taking initiative, practice being an advocate. If you see something that you believe must be done, start doing it even though no one tells you to do so. Don't be afraid of being accused of kissing up for a promotion. Volunteering demonstrates that you are capable and driven.

Develop a habit of taking action. A true leader doesn't stand on the sidelines but is active, dynamic, and a go-getter. You will win trust if you act. No one ever gets praised for doing nothing.

Chapter 11: How to Turn Defeat into Victory

Successful people didn't get to where they are because they never experienced setbacks. All paths are the same. They are filled with hurdles, obstacles, speed bumps and detours. The successful ones don't always win. Once in a while, they experience defeat. But what makes an achiever is his response when he loses. A failure easily surrenders. The achiever chooses to bounce back and move forward.

Setbacks shouldn't be seen as a mere hindrance to success. They have to be learned from. An inventor who doesn't get the result he desires goes back to his methodology and figures out what he did wrong and how to improve it. A football team watches a video of a game that it lost to correct each team member's mistakes. People in every business reconstruct and analyze what went wrong to avoid the same mistakes and improve.

The key point is improvement. Many get so wounded by personal setbacks that they fail to learn from the experience. People fear criticizing themselves. But in order to improve, you first have to know what is wrong. Understand your weaknesses and flaws and then you will find a way to fix them.

*

Accepting praises and taking credit for achievements come easy to most people. They want everyone to know that they are a winner. Nothing is wrong with that. However, most people choose to evade responsibility over a failure; instead, they want to blame something or someone.

Some salesmen blame customers for low sales. Some people who lose a game will accuse others of cheating. Some managers will blame supervisors if projected outputs are not met. There are many who also see bad luck as the cause of their defeat. These are all natural reactions. But take some time to study every setback you encounter and you will realize that you may have caused that defeat yourself.

Don't waste time blaming others. It won't get you anywhere.

*

There are a lot of people who aspire to become writers. But after a few tries, most of them give up when they realize that hard work is required. There are no shortcuts in whatever we undertake, and only persistence keeps us in the game. A few of these writers will persist and persevere and yet not publish anything even after writing hundreds of stories that follow the same formula.

Persistence is an admirable trait. But it alone cannot guarantee success. If that writer continues coming up with the same product which has been rejected time and again, he or she is set up for failure; experimenting with the plot and writing style may lead him or her to come up with something worthy of publication.

Experimentation should be combined with persistence in order to achieve something. If you keep doing the same thing over and over again, your outcome will not change. But don't give up on your goal and use your creative mind to come up with new approaches. Experiment and you will be on your way to success.

Here are two suggestions to develop your power to experiment:

1. Believe that there is a way and that you will find it. If you tell yourself that there's no way out of your problem, you will be convinced that you are defeated. But believe that your problem can be solved and you will find the answers.

2. Press the pause button. Relax your mind for a while. Go out for a walk in the park or take a nap. Start with a refreshed mind and you will figure out new ways.

Finally, see the good side in your defeat. Losing a job is one of the toughest situations you may ever experience. But if that happens, think hard and reflect. Did you really like your job? Did your work provide you with fulfillment? Was it what you needed to reach your life goals? If not, maybe it was time for you to start something new and consider losing your job as a blessing in disguise.

Remember that there is always something good even in the worst situations. You see what you want to see. See the good and turn your defeat into victory.

Chapter 12: Use Goals to Help You Grow

Every success story started as an idea, a visualization that is turned into reality. An idea that is worth pursuing can become a strong goal. However, some people mistake dreams for goals. Dreams remain in a person's mind, but only becomes a goal only when steps are taken to make it come true.

Your goal is where you want to go. Without a goal, you will keep on wandering until your time is up and you realize you have gone nowhere. You must have goals in order to succeed.

Plan. Where do you want to be five or ten years from now? If you want to get somewhere, you should know where you want to go. It doesn't matter where you were or where you are in life right now. You need to set long-term goals in order to grow.

One common problem many people have is that they don't know exactly what they want to do, which causes them to jump from one job to another. With dozens of opportunities available, the possibility of choosing the right one is low. Having a clear vision of yourself at a specific time in the future will guide you what you have to do and help you choose the job that is right for you.

*

One research study determined that people in executive position consistently showed one qualification — the desire to be on top.

Submit yourself completely to your desires. Success requires you to commit your heart, mind, and soul, but you can only do that for something you completely desire.

All of us have desires. But not everyone is able to surrender to them. Many choose the easier path of killing their desires and settling for a mediocre life.

Don't suppress your desires. Believe in what you can do and don't let self-doubt stand in your way. Don't let complacency stop you from not looking for something better. Don't fear competition for the top spot. For younger readers, don't allow your parents dictate what your goals should be. And for those with families, don't use your responsibility as a reason to not change.

Allow your desires to take over you and you will find the energy and enthusiasm to work on your goal. Let your desires absorb you and it'll be easy to find the way and make the right decisions to achieve your goal.

*

You may have spent at least one weekend with no plans at all. It makes you feel light, right? But when you look back on those days, you realize you accomplished nothing and the only time you felt glad was when it finally came to an end. The lesson here is that if you want to achieve something, you must have a specific plan to achieve something.

*

There is no shortcut to success. Progress starts with a single step and the accumulation of these steps is what lead to success. A person trying to quit smoking achieves his ultimate goal not by deciding to never smoke again, but by continuously choosing not to smoke for one hour. Eventually, one hours becomes one day, and one day becomes one week, until he is freed from his habit.

Achieving your goal requires a step-by-step technique. Many times, you will think that you are doing a lot of small tasks which make you feel like you are not getting nearer to where you want to be. Each time you feel that, ask yourself if the task you are doing will help you realize your goals. If not, leave it and continue with the next task. But also remember that each step you take, no matter how insignificant it may seem, gets you closer to your goal.

*

Practice self-investment. How strong a business is years from now does not depend on what it does in the future — it is determined by what it does now. Your life is a business and to make a profit, you should invest in yourself.

76

Investments in education can propel you ahead of the competition. But bear in mind that the number of years you spent in school nor the amount of head knowledge is important — a good education is one that makes you competent and cultivates your mind.

Chapter 13: How to Think Like a Leader

Success goes hand in hand with leadership. You need the ability to lead in order to gain the support of others. Remember that no one will pull you to the top. You have to be lifted by people who work with and for you.

This chapter focuses on the four principles of leadership. Master these and you will find it easy for people to do things for you.

Trade Minds with The People You Want to Influence

Trading minds with others is a sure way to get people to act the way you want them to. Put yourself in their shoes. Use their eyes to see. Consider their interests and you will know how to influence them.

Consider this scenario. An advertisement for a shoe manufacturer is created by John, a well-to-do person who has a sophisticated lifestyle. When creating the commercial, he only considered his own interests. He developed the advertisement for people in a similar income bracket as he without thinking about the rest of the market. In the end, the advertisement failed and the shoe manufacturer's sales didn't increase. Had John put himself in other customers' shoes, the outcome would have been less disastrous.

Remember. When you want someone to do something for you, put yourself in his or her shoes. Ask yourself how you would react if you were him or her. Then act the way that would spur you into action if you were him or her.

Think: What is The Human Way to Handle This?

People have different approaches in terms of leadership. There are those who impose dictatorships, which we all know generally don't last long. Others treat leadership like following a guidebook, not realizing that rules should just be used as a guide; the leader who uses this approach sees people as machines, and people don't like that.

A great leader is someone who employs the "be-human" approach. He or she treats everyone as a human being worthy of respect and tries to help when possible. He or she believes that the people who work for him are his or her responsibility and thus need to be protected. He or she doesn't embarrass or belittle people who make mistakes, but instead works with them to improve and correct their wrongs.

When problems involving your employees arise, consider a humanistic way to deal with these problems. Let people know that you put them first; always treat them well. Show them that you are interested in them. Praise their accomplishments be it on or off the job.

Think Progress, Believe in Progress, Push for Progress

Real leaders have a progressive outlook. To be a great leader, you have to think of improvement and quality in everything you do.

Promotions are always given to those who push for progress. Those who think that everything is going perfectly, that nothing has to be changed, and that the status quo should stay in place, will also remain stagnant. The people who are promoted are those who believe that there is always room for improvement, and provide and implement new ideas that lead to progress.

As a leader, you have great influence in the performance of your followers. They set their standards based on yours. Their actions depend on what you expect of them. They tend to imitate you; they will think, act, and speak the same way you do. Hence, if you want to have a progressive group, become one yourself.

Take Time Out to Confer with Yourself and Tap Your Supreme Thinking Power

With all the responsibilities shouldered by leaders, it is unusual to find one who isn't extremely busy. But unknown to many, they allow themselves alone time with nothing but their thoughts.

Managing alone time is beneficial because it will help you gain a better understanding of yourself. It is a time when you could work out solutions to your problems, plan, or come up with new ideas. Many people fail to tap into their higher-order thinking powers because they consult everybody except themselves. They're afraid of their own thoughts and ideas. In time, they become completely dependent on others. They become someone who doesn't have leader material.

Remember that as a leader, your primary job is to think. Make it a point to have alone time each day to develop your thoughts so you can think yourself to success.

Conclusion

Success is one thing that all people desire. It is their biggest dream. The way to success however is not clear for many — they are not sure what to do or what they need. But what people do not realize is that they have the basic requirement for success — thinking. Everyone has a mind. Everyone has the ability to think. To develop the ability to think big is what will help you succeed.

Believe. Your mind is powerful. You can make the impossible possible if you believe. Believe that you can and your mind will figure out the how. Believe in yourself and other people will have confidence in you.

Avoid making excuses. Health issues should not prevent you from achieving big, nor should your level of intelligence. Remember that you are never too young nor too old to do big things. Don't blame luck if you're not where you want to be, or if others are doing better than you. Success is won and it requires hard work.

Address and destroy your fears because they are the primary enemies of success. Take action to cure fear, as inaction can only worsen it and destroy your confidence.

Think big — the size of your success is proportional to the size of your thinking. Develop the vocabulary of big thinkers by always using positive language. Look beyond what you can see to create a vision of what can be. You may be content where you are but you can always be better.

Be creative. Use your thinking power and believe that you can come up with new ideas and concepts. You have to invent and re-invent in order to keep up with this fast-paced world. Free yourself from the traditional thinking that paralyzes creativity. Ask others for advice and listen to what they have to say; they can provide you with raw material to enhance your creativity.

You are a reflection of your own thoughts. Think that you're important and other people will treat you that way. Think that you deserve respect and you will be respected. Think that you are a winner and you will win.

Your environment is one of your biggest influences in shaping who you are and the size of your thinking. What you are now and what you will be depends on what surrounds you. So, make sure that your environment is working for you.

Develop the right attitude. It will help you win people, become a good leader and it determine the size of your accomplishments. Be enthusiastic and motivate others to do their best. Show others how important they are to you and they will be willing to do more for you. Cultivate a service-first attitude and you see your wealth grow as well.

Treat other people well to win them over. Success is a product of collective effort and you need the support of other people to achieve it. Be likeable. Take initiative when building friendships. Accept differences and always find the good in others.

Great ideas will only have actual value when they are acted upon, so take action. Be someone who does things and gets the desired results. Don't wait until conditions are perfect before you take action unless you want to wait forever. Cultivate initiative and you will find yourself ahead of others.

Do not surrender to defeat. Consider every losing moment as an opportunity to learn and improve. Avoid the habit of blaming others. Sometimes you lose because you only work with persistence; this alone will not guarantee success. Combine persistence with experimentation and you will get results.

Have a clear vision of your goal. Your goal is where you want to go and without it, you will never get anywhere. Know what your desires are and let them drive you to find the enthusiasm to work on your goal.

Think like a leader. Put yourself in other people's shoes and see through their eyes in order to know how to influence them. Be a rational but compassionate leader. Treat everyone with respect and let them know that you are willing to help them any way you can. Have a progressive outlook and always think of quality and improvement. And finally, allow yourself some alone time to enhance your thinking power.

FREE BONUSES

P.S. Is it okay if we overdeliver?

Here at Readtrepreneur Publishing, we believe in overdelivering way beyond our reader's expectations. Is it okay if we overdeliver?

Here's the deal, we're going to give you an extremely condensed PDF summary of the book which you've just read and much more…

What's the catch? We need to trust you… You see, we want to overdeliver and in order for us to do that, we've to trust our reader to keep this bonus a secret to themselves? Why? Because we don't want people to be getting our exclusive PDF summaries even without buying our books itself. Unethical, right?

Ok. Are you ready?

Firstly, remember that your book is code: **"READ105"**.

Next, visit this link: **http://bit.ly/exclusivepdfs**

Everything else will be self explanatory after you've visited: **http://bit.ly/exclusivepdfs.**

We hope you'll enjoy our free bonuses as much as we enjoyed preparing it for you!

Summary:

The Meaning of Marriage

By: Timothy Keller & Kathy Keller

Proudly Brought to you by:

90

Legal & Disclaimer

The information contained in this book is not designed to replace or take the place of any form of medicine or professional medical advice. The information in this book has been provided for educational and entertainment purposes only.

The information contained in this book has been compiled from sources deemed reliable, and it is accurate to the best of the Author's knowledge; however, the Author cannot guarantee its accuracy and validity and cannot be held liable for any errors or omissions. Changes are periodically made to this book. You must consult your doctor or get professional medical advice before using any of the suggested remedies, techniques, or information in this book. Images used in this book are not the same as of that of the actual book. This is a totally separate and different entity from that of the original book titled: "The Meaning of Marriage: Facing the Complexities of Commitment with the Wisdom of God".

Upon using the information contained in this book, you agree to hold harmless the Author from and against any damages, costs, and expenses, including any legal fees potentially resulting from the application of any of the information provided by this guide. This disclaimer applies to any damages or injury caused by the use and application, whether directly or indirectly, of any advice or information presented, whether for breach of contract, tort, negligence, personal injury, criminal intent, or under any other cause of action.

You agree to accept all risks of using the information presented inside this book. You need to consult a professional medical practitioner in order to ensure you are both able and healthy enough to participate in this program.

The Book at a Glance

It is only natural for people in love to get married and start a family. Sadly, the true meaning of marriage had been lost in the passage of time. The modern era has provided us with convenient lives and lesser moral values. Most marriages often end up in divorce, which could negatively affect the lives of children.

The Meaning of Marriage intends to bring back the true meaning of marriage and create a lasting, harmonious relationship between husband and wife. Do your best to make your marriage work for both of you and live the rest of your lives in marital bliss.

The Bible's Ephesians 5 has great marriage passages written by Apostle Paul. Chapter 1 reflects Paul's treatise into the modern cultural context. It also outlines the Bible's most basic teachings on marriage:

> 1. God instituted marriage.
>
> 2. Marriage is a reflection of God's love to deliver salvation to humankind.

Chapter 2 presents Paul's thesis about how married couples

need the guidance of Holy Spirit in their lives. The Holy Spirit gives married couples a divine help against marriage's primary foe known as self-centeredness. Each partner needs the fullness of the Spirit to be able to fulfill their rightful duty and obligation to one another.

Chapter 3 teaches us what marriage is all about, which is love. This chapter will teach you the true meaning of love, the connection between the acts and feelings of love, and relationship between covenantal commitment and romantic passion.

Chapter 4 deals with the question regarding the reason for tying the knot. This chapter will make you see a new and more profound type of happiness that can be found in the distant side of holiness.

Chapter 5 presents the basic skill sets, which can provide immense help along the way.

Chapter 6 is about the Christian teaching regarding the marital union, which should be between two individuals of different sexes. They need to recognize their gender difference as well as learn and mature through it.

Chapter 7 provides valuable help for single individuals to live life to the fullest. They need to think thoroughly with prudence about the kind of marriage that they would like to have later on.

Chapter 8 deals with the issue of intercourse, revealing why the Bible restricts it to marital union and how it will affect life if you choose to tread the path that follows the Bible.

During the time of Genesis, it was normal for men to practice polygamy (the planet only had few people during such time) and people were required by God to propagate and fill the land. Later, the Christian law about marriage was changed. According to it, each man was required to have only one wife.

This book defines marriage as a monogamous, lifelong union. Christianity views marriage as a sacred union between two persons of different genders. It doesn't recognize the marital union of individuals with the same sex. It is the same view that Timothy Keller assumes.

Introduction

William Shakespeare once wrote on Henry V that the best maker of all marriages is God and hearts should be combined as one.

<u>A Book for Married People</u>

When Timothy Keller and his wife began spending time with each other, both of them realized that the other was their heart's rare other half. They met through the author's sister, Susan, who was also a student at the same university as the author. Susan talked to Timothy about Kathy, and vice versa. Kathy urged Susan to recommend one of C.S. Lewis' books to Timothy. The author read it and was moved. Timothy Keller recalled that Lewis mentioned about sharing a "secret thread", which was something that can make individuals share deep friendship or even more.

Did you notice that the books you love so much seem to be connected by a secret thread? You are aware that there's something familiar in all of them that makes you love them, but somehow you could not point it out clearly. It's the same with friendship. You clicked because you were connected by a secret thread. You share common things that drew you closer with one another.

In Timothy and Kathy Keller's case, their friendship grew into something deeper. After the romance, the engagement came naturally. They too had a fragile marriage at first, but their union got stronger as time passed. Before they reached such maturity in their relationship, thousands of hurtful words had been uttered from their mouths. Every now and then, the great debate on dirty diapers would occur. They smashed many wedding chinas and other infamous events had happened before they were able to enjoy marital bliss. They knew that they would face many challenges along the way, but it did not occur to them that marriage could be much harder than they thought.

The Meaning of Marriage is for couples who discovered that married life can be tough. It is for couples who are looking for ways to effectively deal with the fiery matrimony trials and to mature together through them. The book is also for those who regarded the metaphor "the honeymoon is over" as a literal truth.

A Book for Unmarried People

The author believed that modern single people need a

viciously accurate yet glorious foresight about the thing called marriage and what it can be. So, unmarried readers would also benefit from reading the book.

Prior to the actual writing of his book, Timothy Keller read a lot Christian books about marital relationships. Majority of the books were written to address the specific problems of married couples and help them solve their own dilemma. This book has the same goal and its primary objective is to give both married and single people insights on the biblical views of marriage. The views from the Bible can help married couples correct their mistaken beliefs that could be hurting their union. It can also help single people put an end to dismissing or over-desiring marriage. Unmarried readers can benefit a lot from a Bible-based book on marriage because they would be able to get a better idea regarding their prospective partner.

When the author was ministering in the late 1980s in central New York, he and his wife were dumbfounded by the idea that Western culture had regarding marriage. They heard a lot of negative views regarding marriage, including treating it as nothing but a piece of paper. People harbored conflicted emotions from various unfavorable experiences with marriage and raising a family.

In the fall of 1991 in New York, the author preached on marriage and he delivered it in a nine-week series. He began the series by dedicating weeks of lecture on being in a marital relationship to a group on unmarried individuals. The nine-week series became one of the most highly appreciated sermons in the church.

A Book about the Bible

The book is based on the author's personal experience regarding ministry and marriage, but the teachings of the Old and New Testaments were deeply rooted in the pages of the manuscript. Timothy and Kathy Keller were theological students who studied biblical teachings on marriage, gender, and sex. They applied what they learned to their own marriage.

The husband-and-wife pair used their own experience as a married couple and the things they learned from Scripture to instruct, advice, persuade, and guide young adults when it comes to marriage and sex. The Bible doesn't mention anything about how to run schools, hospitals, business establishments, or museums. In fact, there are different human enterprises and institutions that the Bible does not speak of. The people are at liberty to invent and operate these things. Obviously, it is still advisable to follow the general principles stated in the Bible and avoid harming human lives.

God established marriage for the happiness and welfare of people. God created marriage and its design must be regarded with great importance. Those who would like to enter marriage must try to understand its principles. They must humble themselves before God and submit to His purpose.

FREE BONUSES

P.S. Is it okay if we overdeliver?

Here at Readtrepreneur Publishing, we believe in overdelivering way beyond our reader's expectations. Is it okay if we overdeliver?

Here's the deal, we're going to give you an extremely condensed PDF summary of the book which you've just read and much more...

What's the catch? We need to trust you... You see, we want to overdeliver and in order for us to do that, we've to trust our reader to keep this bonus a secret to themselves? Why? Because we don't want people to be getting our exclusive PDF summaries even without buying our books itself. Unethical, right?

Ok. Are you ready?

Firstly, remember that your book is code: **"READ106"**.

Next, visit this link: **http://bit.ly/exclusivepdfs**

Everything else will be self explanatory after you've visited: **http://bit.ly/exclusivepdfs.**

We hope you'll enjoy our free bonuses as much as we enjoyed preparing it for you!

FREE BONUSES

P.S. Is it okay if we overdeliver?

Here at Readtrepreneur Publishing, we believe in overdelivering way beyond our reader's expectations. Is it okay if we overdeliver?

Here's the deal, we're going to give you an extremely condensed PDF summary of the book which you've just read and much more...

What's the catch? We need to trust you... You see, we want to overdeliver and in order for us to do that, we've to trust our reader to keep this bonus a secret to themselves? Why? Because we don't want people to be getting our exclusive PDF summaries even without buying our books itself. Unethical, right?

Ok. Are you ready?

Firstly, remember that your book is code: **"READ106"**.

Next, visit this link: **http://bit.ly/exclusivepdfs**

Everything else will be self explanatory after you've visited: **http://bit.ly/exclusivepdfs**.

We hope you'll enjoy our free bonuses as much as we enjoyed preparing it for you!

Chapter 1: The Secret of Marriage

Ephesians 5:31 to 32 states that a man shall leave the home where he grew up, and live together with his wife and they will become one. It is a profound mystery.

Listening to sentimental marriage talks in Sunday school or church may become a boring subject in the long run. Being in a marital union is glorious but it is also difficult. The married couple may feel fervent joy, but there are times when they need to shed tears, sweat, and blood. They may experience exhausting victories and humbling defeats. Marriage may seem like a fairy tale come true, but only for a few weeks.

There are times that both of you can only rest after a long, difficult day of trying to comprehend what the other thinks or wants to do. You can only grunt that everything is like a profound mystery. At times, you feel like you're in a maze when you're married because you feel like you're losing your way. It's like trying to solve a mysterious puzzle. Despite it all, there's nothing more valuable than marriage among the different types of relationships.

In Genesis 2:22 to 25, it's described how God officiated the first wedding. It's also stated that marriage is the beginning of the most profound association that a person could establish. It is next only to our relationship to God. It is also the reason why knowing and loving your better half can be painful and difficult, and at the same time astounding and rewarding.

The Decline of Marriage

Sadly, marriage continues to decline. Couples just couldn't seem to stay married for so long. The divorce rate is increasing and the number of people getting married is decreasing. The data only show the growing pessimism and wariness regarding marriage that young adults have in the modern time. They believe that the likelihood of landing a good marriage is almost impossible. They also believe that even if they managed to have a stable marriage, there is a horrifying possibility that it may turn out to be sexually boring.

Comedian Chris Rock once asked whether a person wants to be single and pitiful or married and fed up. A number of young adults agreed that the options that Chris Rock presented were the only viable selection. That's why many single people choose something between pure sexual encounters and marriage – living with a sexual partner.

Today, more than half of the population practice

cohabitation before getting married (and some chose not to tie the knot). In the past, cohabitation was practically non-existent. Currently, a quarter of the population of unmarried women between 25 and 39 years old share a home with a partner. One of the reasons for such number is the assumption that most marriages are miserable. Add to that is the fact that almost 50% of all married couples end up divorcing, and many of the remaining 50% just stay together for the sake of their children.

Many argue that cohabiting prior to marriage can help improve the chances of landing a good marriage. It helps the couple discover whether they would be able to click together as married couple or not. It is a chance to know whether the person will remain interesting through the years of being together.

The Surprising Goodness of Marriage

A substantial amount of evidence shows that couples who shared a home together before tying the knot are more likely to split up after they get married. Those who witnessed the painful divorce of their parents regard cohabitation as a practical choice.

It is true that almost 50% of married couples chose to file for divorce when nothing between them seemed to work anymore. However, people overlooked a significant piece of the data. The largest percentage of divorce belongs to the group that got married before they turned 18, had a baby before tying the knot, and dropped out of school.

If the ones living together are already earning decent income, 25 years old and above, come from religious or intact families, and do not have a child out of wedlock, they have a low chance of divorce. They should not worry too much if they decide to settle down. Many young adults prefer cohabitation because they believe that they need to secure their finances first and should already own a home before they marry their partner.

A retirement data study in 1992 showed that individuals who remained married, upon retirement, were richer than those who divorced or remained single. It also showed that married men were able to earn 10% to 40% more than unmarried men who had similar job histories and education.

Marriage can bring a lot of benefits to married couples. They have enhanced physical and mental health, faster equilibrium recovery, and someone to depend on when the going gets tough.

Happily married couples know that they have shared responsibilities and they must do their specific role to the best of their ability to make things work. They save, invest, and think of the other's welfare before their own. These married couples grow and mature as they continue to nurture their feelings for each other. Cohabitation can make partners feel financially secure, but it won't help them grow and reach the level of maturity that they need in order to understand each other better.

The History of Marriage

Most young adults in this modern time have negative beliefs on marriage. Perhaps, the discussions regarding marriage and divorce on different social media have affected or influenced their views. Most talks on the net favor staying single over getting married.

There have been several opposing views about the form and function of marriage in Western civilizations. Take a look at the Protestant and Catholic perspectives. Their views are different in many ways but both believe that marriage is a solemn bond that should create lifelong love and devotion between couples. The bond is a sacrament of God's love and it serves the common good, and Catholics put emphasis on the former while Protestants focus on the latter.

A lifelong marriage is known to create social stability that would be beneficial for child development. Older cultures value the meaning of duty, teaching their members to embrace their roles and fulfill them faithfully – especially when it comes to their role in the family.

In the new approach, marriage is a contract between two parties to fulfill their mutual satisfaction and growth. In this perspective, married persons do not marry to fulfill certain responsibilities to society or God. They married to get themselves some benefits. It's like fulfilling their needs first and taking their spouse's needs for granted.

Tara Parker-Pope of the New York Times says that the practice now is 'me' marriage to obtain a happy marriage. It only means that an individual can only be happy with the marriage when he/she gets the satisfaction that he/she wants to obtain. Nurturing the relationship between husband and wife becomes totally irrelevant.

Parker-Pope also says that the change can be considered revolutionary. Marriage used to cater to the couple's welfare, but now it's only 'me' first.

The Search for a Compatible Soul Mate

David Popenoe and Barbara Dafoe Whitehead wrote on their National Marriage Project of 2002 entitled "Why Men Won't Commit" that upon investigation they found out that the common view of most women regarding men being fearful of marriage had no basis. Their investigation uncovered a striking fact. Many men declared that they wouldn't tie the knot unless they found someone they are compatible with or their perfect soul mate.

When Timothy met Kathy, they found out that they shared a lot of things. They even had the same thoughts about life and other things. They recognized each other as their kindred spirit. However, Popenoe and Whitehead didn't mean the same thing when they talked about the "soul mate" concept. To many young adults, the soul mate they're looking for should be someone that they view to be physically attractive and sexually compatible.

When Popenoe and Whitehead conducted their survey on men, they found out that men were looking for someone who could take them as they are and should not attempt to change them. One man even commented that if they were compatible, it was not necessary to change something just to fit the other party's expectations.

Marriage had been known to turn men into civilized beings. It could be said that one of the traditional purposes of marriage was to change men. Women and men have to consider different issues that affect their thoughts on marriage. One of the life goals of most women is to bear children, and it would be impossible for them to do so when they reach menopausal age. Some women even experienced difficulty conceiving in their 30s or 40s. Men knew that most women tend to worry if their marriage would be postponed further. One man even said that it's a female issue.

Men prefer to delay their marriage and choose cohabitation, which gives them regular access to the sexual and domestic care of a lover while they continue to seek a better partner. Considering the male nature, marriage does not fit any man who considers himself an alpha male.

Men and women of today would like to have a marriage that could give them sexual and emotional satisfaction and let them be themselves. Their spouse should be someone fun to be with and can stimulate their body and brain.

However, in truth, marriage can help men achieve the masculinity they desire. The most valued point of manhood in most Western history was self-mastery. A man who could

112

not control his excessive eating, desire for sex, sleeping, or drinking just failed to rule himself. By extension, he is considered unfit to rule his home. On the other hand, married men are able to establish control over most things in himself and his household.

The Irony of Pessimistic Idealism

In the past, talks about finding an ideal soul mate and ensuring compatibility were uncommon. Today, men and women are looking for a partner who is willing to accept them and able to fulfill their desires. Such way of thinking only generates a set of unrealistic expectations that could lead to disappointment.

The internet, MTV, and televised specials of Victoria's Secret could be responsible for most men's reason to delay their marriage with their girlfriend because they hope to find a soul mate or babe that would satisfy their requirements. Hoping too much creates fanatical idealism. When it takes too long to meet one's ideal, pessimism sets in.

You may set some standards for your ideal mate, but you want your partner to accept you as you are. Making a compromise seems to be impossible if your way of thinking is such. The reality is your ideal person may have some flaws that must be changed or you can just accept that person as he is. On the other hand, you are not so perfect yourself. You may need to change something in you to fit perfectly with your potential partner.

No matter how you look at it, extreme idealism would only lead to utter frustration.

You Never Marry the Right Person

If you never or didn't marry the right person, what can you do? It is best to find the answer in the Bible. It explains why it's futile to seek a partner that you can be compatible with. The Bible says love should come unpretentiously.

A person who has too many requirements in finding the right person and still married someone who did not fully meet the conditions would naturally conclude that he/she did not marry the right person. To be blunt, no one is certain who they marry.

The person you married or are going to marry may not be the right person at the time of marriage, but it doesn't mean that it would remain that way for the rest of your lives. Remember that marriage can help nurture feelings and allow both parties to mature and grow.

Chapter 2: The Power for Marriage

Ephesians 5:21 says that husband and wife should submit themselves to one another in respect for Christ.

Be Filled with the Spirit

Apostle Paul described many marks of an individual "filled with the Spirit", which was the last clause in verse 21 of Ephesians 5 in Greek text. A person could humbly serve others if he/she set aside his/her self-will and pride. After discussing this in depth, Paul continued with the roles of husbands and wives.

The word "submit" had drawn the attention of modern Western readers because it had something to do with gender roles. Paul was trying to point out that married couples should learn to serve others under the guidance of the Holy Spirit and acquire the power to confront marital difficulties.

In John 14:17 and 26, Jesus described the Holy Spirit as the "Spirit of truth". It would serve as a reminder regarding everything that Jesus had said. The task of the Holy Spirit in such case was to uncover the meaning of Jesus' work and persona to believers.

To be filled with the Spirit is to live a joyful life.

<u>Submit to One Another</u>

Having the ministry of Spirit in your relationship as husband and wife can help you deal with the challenges of marital union. In verses 22 to 24 of Ephesians 5, a wife was told to submit to her husband. Immediately after that, a husband was told to love his wife as Christ loves the congregation. The husband should remain faithful to his wife. Being husband and wife means living for one another, which is the most difficult to do yet is the most important function of being a better half.

Christians who were able to bring about radical change were the ones who fully grasped the gospel. Paul did not say that we should force ourselves to embrace the idea that others are always better than us. When he mentioned about us being servants to one another, it was not a literal master-servant relationship. In Paul's explanation, being a servant to one another meant putting that person's needs first.

Marriage can only thrive when both husband and wife have the servant attitude, which Paul mentioned. It may be difficult at first, but both parties will eventually get used to it. Understand that it requires the Spirit of Truth in the Holy

116

Spirit for us to serve another human being. The gospel must be driven into the heart and allow it to create the change naturally.

The Problem of Self-Centeredness

Radical self-centeredness had always been the primary hindrance in the attempt to develop a servant heart. Self-centeredness brought a lot of problems to married couples in the past. It still brings the same set of problems today.

1 Corinthians 13 gave a great description of love that everyone should keep in their heart. Love is the reverse of "self-seeking". The married couple's discord is often caused by the other or both parties' self-centeredness. However, the gospel can help the husband and wife attain happiness by humbling themselves and allowing them to gain satisfaction from their relationship. The moment they have finally driven self-centeredness out of their path, the happiness in front of them becomes totally visible.

The Wounds We Carry

Different people have different emotional wounds from past experiences. The wound is a mixture of disillusionment, resentment, guilt, and self-doubt. That wound may never go away even if one marries. When conflicts between husband

and wife occur, the wound may likely re-open and intensify an already heated argument. Couples may become insensitive at such point. The wounds and pain can make self-centeredness more obstinate.

Confronting Our Self-Centeredness

Because everyone inherited the sins of Adam and Eve, it's easier to nurture self-centeredness than adopt the ways of the servant. Jesus died for us so we would no longer live for ourselves but for the Christ.

In today's Western culture, many people get married when they feel a strong attraction to the other party. They believe that they are marrying a wonderful person. After a month or so, the flaws begin to emerge and selfishness is one of the subjects that couples commonly mention.

The best thing that married couples should do is take a look at their own selfishness and treat it as the main cause of problem in the relationship. Each party should seriously consider the teachings of the Bible.

It Only Takes One to Begin Healing

It isn't necessary for both parties to admit that their own selfishness causes the problem – one is enough. If you have decided to be the one to face the burden, you must be ready to do something about your selfishness. Your spouse may not show any response at first, so you need to be patient. Soon, your good behavior and attitude will change your spouse's disposition.

In due time, the other party will realize that he/she must also do something to make the marriage work. Those who stopped pouring their energy into thinking how unhappy they were in their marriage suddenly felt that their coveted happiness had finally arrived at their doorstep. They only need to welcome it wholeheartedly and watch it grow.

The Fear of Christ

In the Old Testament, it is common to see the term "the fear of the Lord". Fear could mean a lot of different things. Fear could be synonymous with being scared or terrified. You show your respect when you fear someone. Fear can also manifest when you think that you might disappoint your important person. You fear the Lord and God because you are overwhelmed by their love and greatness. The more we get to feel and see God's forgiveness and grace, the more we tremble in awe.

Displaying our fear before Christ means bowing to him to

show respect and appreciation for everything he did for us. To reciprocate the things that have been bestowed upon us, it is only right to keep the fruits of Spirit do wonders in our lives.

Chapter 3: The Essence of Marriage

Genesis 2:24 puts emphasis on the reason why a man should leave his mother and father and be with his wife to become one flesh.

<u>Love and the "Piece of Paper"</u>

The author remembered a movie he watched in the past. A man and a woman were already cohabiting and they were arguing over the suggestion of the man to get married. The woman told the man that a piece of paper was not needed in order for her to love him.

The statement that the woman gave had stuck to the author. She was implying that the piece of paper did nothing to enhance the love she had for the man. On the contrary, that piece of paper may hurt them. For years, the author kept hearing the same line from young adults.

According to the Bible, love must be measured according to the person's willingness to give him or herself to someone and not the other way around. Most young people today believe that romantic love is important but never lasts. Due to this understanding, they look at a contract of marriage as a mere paper that would only complicate things. The contract binds the couple together, and then they need to go through the excruciating divorce process when they can no longer tolerate each other's company.

The Overly Subjective View of Love

The expression of love out of obligation is unhealthy to a married couple's relationship. People believe that it's oppressive and inauthentic to have sex for your spouse's satisfaction even though you're not enthusiastic about it. These people argue that both parties should be "in the mood" to make love. However, most couples won't always be in the mood at the same time. When they wait until both of them feel like doing it, their bedroom business most likely gets terminated prematurely. It will surely affect their relationship.

Sex should not be taken as a means to impress your partner. Forbidden and dangerous sex should not be mistaken for love. Being intimate, even though one or both parties are not in the mood, could improve the relationship.

Consumer or Covenant?

Love should be more on doing things than just feeling it. Married couples should always think about each other's welfare before their own.

Consumer relationships had always been there throughout history. That kind of relationship is not long lasting because the consumer will only patronize a particular vendor as long as the price remains satisfactory. In a consumer relationship, the needs of a person are more significant than the relationship itself.

Covenantal relationships, on the other hand, are more focused on the welfare of the relationship than the needs of a person. A covenantal relationship is also binding.

Covenants are mentioned throughout the Bible. Between human beings there were "horizontal" covenants, which close friends share. The covenants between God and individuals were referred to as "vertical" covenants.

Among the covenantal relationships, marriage is the most profound. Marriage possesses strong vertical and horizontal covenants.

Today, most people nurture and appreciate consumer relationships more than covenant relationships, which is slowly disappearing in our time.

The Power of Promising

Divorce has always been and will always be difficult for all the people involved. Marriage vows can help fortify the relationship between husband and wife. The vows must be uttered wholeheartedly and should not be just for show to complete the wedding ceremony. Solemn marriage vows can help the married couples stay true to their promise and do their best to nurture their love and passion while having a servant attitude.

To have a successful marriage, everything must be balanced. It should not always be all action or all emotion. Though couples must be clear regarding their duties, they should also take time to fully appreciate each other's presence and the things that their partner has given. Some compromise must be made in order to achieve a harmonious relationship. Above anything else, husband and wife must keep the vows they uttered on their wedding day and make sure to spend each day happily.

Chapter 4: The Missions of Marriage

Ephesians 5:25 to 27 urge husbands to love their wives the way Christ loves the church, and to keep themselves blameless and holy.

Loneliness in Paradise

What is marriage for? You already know what marriage is, but what is its purpose? The foundation of marriage is friendship. When God created the first man, Adam, He created a perfect world for Adam to live in. God noticed that Adam was not happy despite the fact that he was in paradise. God created a companion, a friend (we know as Eve) for Adam to ease his loneliness. In Genesis 5:16, Adam said that his companion was his friend and lover.

The Character of Friendship

The Bible, especially the Book of Proverbs, gave hefty definitions of all sorts of friends. There are real friends and fake friends. There are friends who will love you for all times, and there are also those who will immediately leave you when you can no longer offer benefits.

A real friendship offers transparency and constancy. A real friend has the ability to make you feel safe and secure, will never let you down, will give you a push when you need it, and will be there for you no matter what. A real friendship has common passion. Remember the secret thread? When you meet someone who shares the same thread with you, the blossoming of real friendship is possible – but you need to nurture it with constancy and transparency.

People who believe in Christ share the same secret thread despite their differences in personal history, race, culture, temperament, and social status. They know that God's grace is true and put their faith in Jesus' gospel. A real, robust friendship between two Christians that share the same faith in Christ is possible. They have spiritual transparency as well as spiritual constancy.

<u>Your Spouse as Your Best Friend</u>

Adam knew that Eve was his and regarded her as his friend and lover that filled the void in his heart. There was an era when a married woman was treated as mere property of her husband and not a friend and "co-worker". Marriages in that era were also regarded as business deals among families that could provide security and enhanced social status.

Most people these days put emphasis on sex and romance. In tribal societies, social status is more important than romance.

126

In most Western societies, great sex and romance are more important than anything else. They completely ignore the importance of romance or the responsibility to the community. Marriage also means companionship in the Bible's view. The people in the mentioned societies put more importance on the worldly benefits that they could attain from marrying someone than on the lifelong friendship they would get from the relationship.

If the reason for marriage is to enhance social status, that marriage is doomed from the start because socio-economic status always changes. If the reason for marriage is based on physical attraction and sexual chemistry, then that marriage is bound to end soon when physical attractiveness has waned. Either reason isn't good because they only create a fragile marital bond that may not even last a decade.

Jesus had shown how a friend should behave. He never let anyone down and he was always there for someone to lean on. If the married couple has Jesus in their lives, they would be able to behave according to Jesus' ways and be each other's best friend who selflessly thinks about goodness and welfare.

When looking for a potential marriage partner, most people tend to search for a finished statue rather than a magnificent block of marble. During Michelangelo's time, someone asked how he carved his famous statue of David and he replied that he just removed the parts that did not belong to David. In the same manner, those looking for a marriage partner must analyze the person from the inside and witness how God brings out the goodness of that potential partner.

Everyone has flaws due to the original sin, which was committed by Adam and Eve. Everyone has their own weaknesses. If the couples have God in their relationship, they will be able to gain insights on how to be each other's strength.

A Message for Our Culture

Most people will surely agree that there's hint of the truth in men giving beauty the top priority when looking for a wife, and that women prefer a financially stable (or wealthy) husband. However, anyone who thinks that way will be lonely in the end. Even though Adam was already living in paradise, he was still lonely. He needed a companion and not just a sexual partner.

Your marriage is bound to end the moment your spouse sensed that you have selfish reasons for marrying. It only proves that you don't give importance to the person at all and are only after the benefits that you will gain from the marriage. You need to make your marriage your top priority. No other person should receive more devotion, energy, diligence, and love than your better half.

Chapter 5: Loving the Stranger

It is written in Ephesians 5:25 to 26 that the man gave himself up for the woman to make her holy by cleansing her using the water through the word.

The truth is none of us know who we are going to marry even if we feel like we do. Sometimes, the person whom you think you know very well suddenly becomes a stranger right before your eyes after being married to him or her for a period of time. Marriage can change a person so as having children and other things along the way, including ageing and career shifts.

Most people get married because they are in-love, which could lead to obsession. Gary Chapman, an author and marriage counselor, believes that the "in-love" phase usually lasts up to a maximum of two years. During such time, a beloved may seem like a deity in the eyes of the person in-love. When it's over, the deity becomes a stranger. It's like they know they married the right person but then he/she has turned into someone unfamiliar. It's like it's the same body with a different soul.

The Power of Truth – Facing the Worst

Everyone is wearing a mask. There are certain things about us that we don't want other people to know. However, marriage strips off that mask and sooner or later, your spouse will see the person that you really are. In marriage, you are totally exposed. You both live under one roof and will see each other's unguarded moments even if you both try to hide something from each other. Your partner will eventually learn of your habits and mannerisms. Both of you will be forced to face the sins and flaws of each other.

Your parents, siblings, and close friends may have seen your flaws and did not mind too much. However, it is different between husband and wife. If either or both of you have a tendency to hold grudge, it's possible that every argument means another plot to get even. Your spouse is supposed to be your best friend, but that would be impossible if trust is already lost.

Marriage has the intrinsic ability to show the true nature of both parties. Marriage may reveal your unflattering, pragmatic side. It may seem like dispiriting but it is also liberating. If you keep denying that flaw in your character, it will soon dominate you. Marriage can help both husband and wife to stop criticizing each other, and to work together to point out

131

and correct each other's flaws. When you give your partner the right to help you, it won't be long before you become best of friends.

"Someone Better" is Your Spouse

Somehow, your feelings get affected when you begin to see each other's flaws. You just can't seem to look at your spouse with the same affection as you did before. When things become tough, some people flee the marriage and there are others that still try to salvage the relationship. Should you find somebody better when the marriage seems to fall apart? Won't you do anything to save it?

When you want to find somebody better, you only need to look at your spouse and try to see the future version of that person. Help him or her be a better person than he/she is today. Try to be the wind beneath each other's wings and reach for your dreams together.

The Power of Love – Renewing the Heart

Marriage has the power to expose who you really are, with all your imperfections revealed before your spouse. Marriage joins together two lives as one. Marriage should make one realize that he/she is stuck to his or her spouse for life. Couples should let their love grow with them as they mature.

Instead of blaming each other, they need to try their best to renew their hearts and live together harmoniously.

God's love for us is so immense that it covered our sins and He continues to accept us despite our faults. As a married couple, you need to strengthen your love to each other so you can accept your partner's flaws, reprogram him or her, and continue to shower your spouse with your deep affection.

When you love your spouse, love him or her with all your heart. Keep the servant attitude in mind and serve your spouse to the best of your ability. Remember that he/she is not someone else, but your best friend.

The Power of Grace – Reconciling

Jesus mentioned in Mark 11:25 that when you realized that you hold a grudge against someone while saying your prayer, you must forgive that person before continuing. It doesn't mean that you shouldn't confront that person. Galatians 6 and Matthew 18 states that if someone has wronged you, it's best to have a talk with the involved party and discuss the wrong things that he/she did to you. Settling things amicably is still better than plotting revenge, especially if the other party is your spouse. Set things straight, forgive the wrong doings, and let your love grow.

Chapter 6: Embracing the Other

Ephesians 5:22 to 23 and 25 states that the head of a wife is her husband, and she should surrender herself to her spouse. The head of the church is Christ. Husbands must love their wives in the same manner that Christ loves the church.

Most women nowadays fight for equality in almost everything they do – career, view, power, and others. When there's talk about marriage, roles of husband and wife as well as children are commonly discussed. In our modern time, traditional views regarding the roles of the parties involved are being altered. Various groups that fight for equality believe that men and women should be given equal roles. It is also possible that they refuse to accept that a wife should submit to her husband as the Bible says.

In the Beginning

From the start, God made us male or female. The body of each gender is uniquely designed. Regardless of gender, everyone is equal in the eyes of God. Adam and Eve were created in God's image and the same goes with every human being. The first man and woman were tasked to be fruitful and fill the land. The gift to procreate is something that only a man and woman can carry out. The verses strongly suggest

135

that both genders are complementary, and they have the same worth and dignity.

Adam is Eve's physical source and was responsible for naming her. These elements lay the basis regarding the headship of a husband. Even though the authority was given to the man, the woman was not described as someone inferior. She was properly described as a suitable helper. The Hebrew used the term "ezer" that means a kind of helper that can fill the gap in fulfilling certain tasks. Eve was the only suitable being that could properly help Adam with his tasks.

Man and woman are similar to two puzzle pieces that fit together. The absence of the other won't complete the whole picture.

But What About Headship?

When Adam and Eve were banished from paradise, they began to blame each other and needed to do everything in their power to survive. However, they still lived together and tried to raise their growing family.

The restoration of love and unity between man and woman happened during Jesus' time. He also redeemed the servant-head and "ezer"-subordinate roles of married couples. When

Jesus was sent to deliver mankind to salvation, he set aside his divine privileges and assumed the role of a servant. However, he did not become less divine. He had been patient and humble when teaching his people and dealing with his enemies.

In the modern time, some women who hold key positions in the company they work for may find it hard to submit themselves to their husbands. A woman who has a number of subordinates might find it difficult to willingly submit to her husband.

A woman should also understand that although men are the head, they have a servant-head role. It is written in John 13: 12 to 16 that Jesus humbled himself by washing the feet of the people who were calling him Lord and teacher. He told them that he had set an example to humble themselves before others. Husbands are expected to follow Jesus' example. Although a husband is the head of his wife and the entire family, he should also assume the traits of a servant.

Jesus displayed his sacrificial submission and sacrificial authority before his people. Both men and women should learn from Jesus' example and accept gender roles wholeheartedly.

<u>Embracing the Other</u>

Men and women have distinguishable calls and they possess distinguishable abilities to help them perform their specific tasks. A woman's body has the ability to bear children. A man is usually stronger than a woman and is more adept at doing physical labor. There are other things that only men or women can do. In almost all things, they complement each other. One task cannot be completed without the assistance of the other. Take procreation as an example.

The full embrace of the other gender can only happen in marriage. Men and women are completely different yet won't be able to function fully without the other.

Chapter 7: Singleness and Marriage

Paul wrote in 1 Corinthians 7 that an unmarried man should not look for a wife. If he decided to get married, he did not commit a sin. A virgin that got married had not sinned.

When you continue to read the passage, Paul further explains that married couples will deal with many difficulties and he wants to spare single people the trouble. He added that time is short.

Even today, the passage is quite confusing if you don't try to analyze it carefully. The Old Testament prophets preached that the old order would soon end upon the arrival of the Messiah. Imagine the surprised expression of everyone when no throne ascending occurred and the Messiah was sentenced to death. He did not bring judgment upon mankind but instead, delivered us to salvation.

The Goodness of Singleness

Jesus and Paul were unmarried their whole lives. There were other ardent followers of Jesus who chose to remain single and decided to devote their time in spreading the teachings of gospel.

According to the Bible, singleness is a noble condition that

God has bestowed. In various circumstances, being unmarried is actually better than being married. Christians in the past, who remained unmarried, stated that the future could only be guaranteed by God and not the family. The said Christians put their hope in God and no one else. Unmarried Christians from the past and present will always have fathers and mothers as well as brothers and sisters in Christ.

Western culture entices us to believe in apocalyptic romance in which a perfect mate is the one that can bring utter emotional and spiritual fulfillment. Numerous cultural narratives that follow Disney-style storytelling convey a single message – in life, the most important things are finding romance and marrying your significant other. Western and traditional cultures view singleness as a condition that can be regarded as something subhuman and grim.

Unmarried Christians who may want to remain that way are able to nurture a fulfilling, deep relationship with Jesus. Of course, they may still dream of getting married, but they don't pressure themselves to find someone.

The Goodness of Seeking Marriage

Even though Christians view singleness as something good, it does not mean that they want to avoid marriage. Most unmarried people in today's society have this misery of having little desire to get married since they're afraid of the changes or things that might occur.

Traditional societies tend to value marriage too much, while contemporary societies will likely give importance on independence. People from traditional societies get married to improve their status, find stability, and fulfill their duty. People from contemporary societies get married to satisfy personal fulfillment. Both motives are only partially right, but they can become the definitive goal if the gospel fails to change the heart and mind of a person.

History of Dating

In America during ancient times up to 19th century, arranged marriages were an ordinary occurrence. Back then, people belonged to traditional societies and so, they would naturally follow marriage customs.

During the late 19th century, a system of "calling" or courtship was born. Love became the dominant reason for marriage. When a man was invited to call on the woman, he was expected to spend time together with her in the woman's family parlor or front porch. The man was literally invited into the woman's home and they get to know each other better together with the woman's family. Inviting men to call was the lady's privilege. When there was love between both parties, they could decide to get married.

In the early 20th century, young men and women began to practice modern "dating". It was pretty much the same as today's dating but more conservative. Before, the focus of dating was getting to know each other's character and establishing friendship. Today, most dating couples are more focused on having fun, being seen, and spending cash.

The "hook-up" culture emerged in the 21st century. According to the New York Times, teenagers find dating to be troublesome. However, they are aware that dating is important in building a marital relationship. A hook-up is a plain sexual encounter with no strings attached. After a hook-up, the couple may decide to start dating, meet one more time, or never see each other again.

There are numerous religious communities that try to bring back the community and family involvement in the search for a partner. There are Christian communities that try to bring back the marriage pathways of the past. Some even suggest that the woman's father should choose the marriage partner for his daughter.

Some Practical Counsel for Marriage Seekers

Some people think that marriage is a sort of escape route, especially for individuals who feel safe and secure if they have someone to rely on. Paul regarded singleness as a gift because a person will not have a wish to be married, experience restlessness, or go through emotional struggle. However, this doesn't mean that every person who lacks romantic desire has received a gift from God. There are several dreadful reasons for not marrying, including disregard for the opposite sex, failure to keep friends, and a selfish spirit.

Singleness, as being a gift that Paul mentioned, had something to do with his freedom to focus deeply on his ministry, which was something impossible for a married man to accomplish. Paul valued the fruitfulness of his ministry and life. It was all thanks to his singleness.

Young people nowadays go on a date to have someone to accompany them to events, concerts, and others. They have no intention to deepen the relationship or marry. An older person who has a plan to get married should treat dating as a way to get to know the potential partner better and see if they can make things work between the two of them. With those in mind, here's a list of advice:

143

1. Act according to your age.

2. Avoid having deep emotional involvement with a non-believer.

3. Never allow your passion find its fulfillment before saying your marriage vows.

4. Never let things become too passionate within a short period of time.

5. Respect and take into account the suggestions from friends, family, and the Christian community regarding a potential partner.

Christians should find ways to invite each member of their Christian community into their homes without trying to hide anything regarding the difficult and glorious things that marriage can bring.

Chapter 8: Sex and Marriage

Ephesians 5:31 specifically tells a man to leave his parents and be with his wife to become one flesh.

In this regard, it is impossible to discuss marriage without mentioning intimacy. It is important for each person to understand the Biblical sex ethic – being intimate or having sex should be an exclusive activity between a married couple.

Sex is Just an Appetite; No, It's Not

All throughout history, there had been different perceptions about sex. Some people believe that sex is an appetite that must be satisfied when needed. Some people view sex like a cuisine that must have varying taste in order to be truly enjoyable. There are people who believe that limiting sex is unhealthy.

There are others who view sex as something dirty and taboo. For them, it is something degrading and evil.

There are also people who regard sex as some kind of self-expression. You may treat it as a way to find yourself and be yourself. The primary function of sex, in this case, is for self-realization and fulfillment in whatever way he/she wants to engage in.

Sex is an appetite that is different from our need to sleep or eat. Sex can somehow influence not just the person's body but also the heart and inner self. In the Christian view, sex must only be done between husband and wife and no one else.

Sex is Dirty; No, It's Not

The Bible contains sensible explanations and accounts that can convince anyone that sex is neither dirty nor bad. To maintain the sanctity of intimacy, however, the act should only be done within marriage. To be blunt, engaging in sexual intercourse outside of marriage makes the act dirty.

Understand that sex is not about pleasure or duty. When a person marries, he/she creates a solemn covenant with his/her spouse. When the Bible speaks of "covenant partner", it pertains to your spouse (as mentioned in Proverbs 2:17). The married couple becomes one flesh and should take good care of each other's body as if it's their own. Both parties need to make sure that they won't bring harm upon each other's body and maintain the covenant. Having an illicit affair is considered dirty and it breaks the covenant between husband and wife.

Like most people, Christians have their moments of

weakness or vulnerability (due to certain circumstances). During such times, a person could be easily persuaded to do sexual acts outside of marriage. A surefire way of avoiding such temptation is to have a strong connection with Christ. There are also times when you just can't seem to free your mind of sexual thoughts and desires. You need to do your best to strike a balance to such desires and thoughts by recalling the gospel and keeping yourself busy with worthwhile activities.

The Importance of Erotic Love in Marriage

Don't be surprised to read numerous passages that tell husband and wife to take pleasure in sex and frequently do the act. Proverbs 5:19 tells a husband to find delight in the body of his wife and no one else. Paul also provided a positive view of sexual pleasure within marriage.

1 Corinthians 7 states that when it comes to intimacy, each spouse's main concern should be giving sexual pleasure to his or her partner and not getting it. In other words, seeing your spouse enjoying the intimacy should be your greatest sexual pleasure. If your spouse demands more sex than you, then you can treat sexual intimacy as your gift to your partner when your spouse give hints that he/she wants to do it.

147

Conclusion

The Meaning of Marriage reveals the truth about marriage – it's not a fairytale where the main characters get married and live happily ever after. On the contrary, you and your spouse are going to embark on a new journey and experience new adventure that only both of you, as married couple, must face. The person you married may not be the right person at the time when you walked down the aisle and uttered your marriage vows. In due time and after being together as you nurture your relationship with Christ, you will discover that nobody is more suitable to be your spouse than the one you married some time ago.

Married couples should learn to nurture the fruits of Spirit and submit to one another. As a married couple, you both need to cultivate the servant attitude and live together harmoniously. It is advisable to choose a covenantal relationship, as it is known to last. Your family will soon grow bigger with the addition of the little ones, whom can bring joy to your lives and complete your existence.

You both need to treat one another as each other's best friend. You must try to create a transparent and constant friendship in order to maintain peace and harmony in your relationship. Remember that doubt can ruin your relationship

– and no one would want that to happen. When doubt creeps in, your relationship becomes vulnerable and you may end up falling apart. Settle things amicably right away to avoid shattering your relationship.

Think of your spouse as someone better than you and give him/her the respect that he/she deserves. Too much pride can also tear you apart. You need to treat each other as the puzzle piece that makes each one of you complete. You may be different from each other but you complement and complete each other. It would be impossible for either of you to function fully without the other.

Nonetheless, let us not forget that singleness is a gift as it provides freedom to focus on ministry. Not every person can have such gift. On the other hand, marriage is considered glorious. Those who got married or plan to get married must do everything in their power to make things work. Married life is challenging, but a couple who nurtures and cultivates the things that can help make marriage work can look forward to a blissful union.

As a married couple, you both should learn more about giving pleasure to the other. Never forget the servant attitude, which Christ himself had shown.

Marriage should have love, friendship, romantic passion, a servant attitude, and Christ to function well. There will be trials or obstacles in your relationship, but you will be able to conquer them with God's help. As husband and wife, you should continue living your lives according to the teachings of the Bible and make Christ the center of your marriage.

Epilogue

Understand that marriage does not encompass just one form of human love. It's not limited to passionate romance, friendship, servitude, or sense of duty. It is all those things and even more. Marriage can be overwhelming.

George Herbert, a 17th century Christian poet composed three love poems. The most famous was *Love (III)*.

The first stanza narrates how Love called upon the lyrical voice or the guest. Love is being personified as something that can communicate with the lyrical voice, portraying the way humans interact with each other. It is, at the same time, a God metaphor. However, the lyrical voice felt guilty and wanted to turn down the invitation of Love. Instead of criticizing or blaming the guest, Love asked if he/she wanted to obtain something. The lyrical voice was ashamed of his/her sins.

The guest further stated that he/she couldn't even look upon Love. It was later revealed that the mysterious figure was the one who made the guest's eyes and he/she came to realize who Love was and he/she called him Lord. In the end, the lyrical voice was able to cast aside his/her feelings of guilt and embraced the Lord's gentle words.

1 John 4 gives us a warm reminder to love one another because God gave His love to us. He who does not know how to love will never get to know God, who is the perfect personification of love. God lives in every fiber of our being and His love made us whole.

APPENDIX: Decision Making and Gender Roles

The following principles can help married couples in their everyday lives:

- The husband should always think of the interests of his wife. His headship does not mean controlling or maneuvering his family to the direction that he alone decides. It does not give him the authority to get his way in each argument. In Romans 15:2 and 3, Jesus did nothing to please himself. On the other hand, Ephesians 5:21 shows how Jesus, as a servant-leader, made some sacrifices.

- A wife is not merely a follower but a co-worker. She is her husband's most trusted friend. Together they complete and complement each other.

- A wife should respect and submit to her husband's headship, but should not do things that God forbids. If her husband is making her do things against the will of God, she should not follow her husband. She is not being disrespectful of her husband's authority when she refuses to do things that defy God.

153

- The husband being the head of his wife and family is done only for purposes of ministering the household. He can subdue his wife if her choices or decisions prove to be destructive.

- Couples should do their best to achieve marital bliss. Problems and challenges are bound to occur, and that's why it is important to learn how to get along well.

About the Authors

Timothy Keller was born and grew up in Pennsylvania. He went to Westminster Theological Seminary, Gordon-Conwell Theological Seminary, and Bucknell University. He was once a pastor in Hopewell, Virginia. By 1989, in New York City, he established the Redeemer Presbyterian Church with his wife and children.

Today, the church that the Kellers established has five thousand plus attendees every Sunday. Around the world, it has almost two hundred new churches.

Kathy Keller was raised outside Pittsburgh, Pennsylvania. She led Christian fellowship groups when she was still attending Allegheny College. She met Timothy Keller when she attended Gordon-Conwell Theological Seminary.

When their final semester was about to begin, Kathy and Timothy decided to get married. In 1975, at Gordon-Cornwell, Kathy received her MA in Theological Studies. The couple moved to Virginia where Timothy became a pastor in West Hopewell Presbyterian Church, which was his first church. Their children were born there. Nine years later, the Kellers moved to New York and the Redeemer Presbyterian Church was established.

FREE BONUSES

P.S. Is it okay if we overdeliver?

Here at Readtrepreneur Publishing, we believe in overdelivering way beyond our reader's expectations. Is it okay if we overdeliver?

Here's the deal, we're going to give you an extremely condensed PDF summary of the book which you've just read and much more…

What's the catch? We need to trust you… You see, we want to overdeliver and in order for us to do that, we've to trust our reader to keep this bonus a secret to themselves? Why? Because we don't want people to be getting our exclusive PDF summaries even without buying our books itself. Unethical, right?

Ok. Are you ready?

Firstly, remember that your book is code: **"READ106"**.

Next, visit this link: **http://bit.ly/exclusivepdfs**

Everything else will be self explanatory after you've visited: **http://bit.ly/exclusivepdfs.**

We hope you'll enjoy our free bonuses as much as we enjoyed preparing it for you!